A Question of Science

Why is ice slippery?

and other questions about MATERIALS

Anna Claybourne

WAYLAND
www.waylandbooks.co.uk

First published in Great Britain in 2020
by Wayland

© Hodder and Stoughton, 2020

Credits:
Editor: Julia Bird
Design and illustrations: Matt Lilly
Cover design: Matt Lilly

HB ISBN 978 1 5263 1164 1
PB ISBN 978 1 5263 1165 8

Printed and bound in China

MIX
Paper from
responsible sources
FSC® C104740

Picture credits:

Dreamstime: Eknarin Maphichai 17tl; Felix Pergande 25c.
Science Photo Library: Natural History Museum London 19b; Javier
Trueba/MSF 19c.
Shutterstock: Africa Studio 17tr, 20tl, 22clr, 22cr; Waqar Ahmed 86
18t; Tommy Alven 21t; Willyam Bradberry 26t; Captureandcompose
4bl; Chones 21t 26-27; Marcel Clemens 12br; CWIS 15t; Demidoff
27c; Djgis 26c; Dimmber 6cl; George Dolgikh 12cr; Domnitsky
4c; Dreamsquare 22br; Angela Dukich 25t; Engraving Factory
4bc; Fotokostic 20cl; Hekla 28t; Anton Herrington 23b; Hidesy 8c;
Hortimages 10b; Palmer Kane LLC 16cl; Kertu 28b; Chris Kolaczan
19t; Peter Kotoff 29t; Olha Kozachenko 17b; Gita Kulinitch Studio 4bcr;
Andrey_Kuzmin 4cl, 8t, 10t, 22cl; Macrowildlife 4cr; Alexander Mak
27l; mamma_mia 20cr; MIA Studio 16cr; Militarist 5tr; Nattika 21cr;
Nyura 18c; Mike_O 22clc; Hoha-OLD 6t; Patpitchaya 29c; Picador
Pictures 17cr; Kittiphong Phongaen 4br; Photka 4clc; Photographicss
4bcl; rCarner 8b; Will Rodrigues 9t; Sashkin 22bc; Sebastian Studio
18b; Snehit Photo 5l; Sportpoint 6cr; Bernhard Staehli 25b; Sunny
Forest 12bl; Angelus_Svetlana 27r; TaraPatta 21cl; Igor Tarasyuk 12c;
TravnikovStudio 4t; Vector Pattern 17c; WDG Photo 24; Xpixel 17cl,
21b, 26b; Vasilyev: 19t; Yeti studio 1,12cl.

Every effort has been made to clear copyright.
Should there be any inadvertent omission, please apply
to the publisher for rectification

Wayland
An imprint of
Hachette Children's Group
Part of Hodder and Stoughton
Carmelite House
50 Victoria Embankment
London EC4Y 0DZ

An Hachette UK Company
www.hachette.co.uk
www.hachettechildrens.co.uk

Contents

What are materials?

Reach out and feel whatever's around you. Is it a book, your clothes, a chair or sofa, a snack? Or maybe you're on a beach, surrounded by rocks and sand. Well, wherever you are, you wouldn't be there if it weren't for materials.

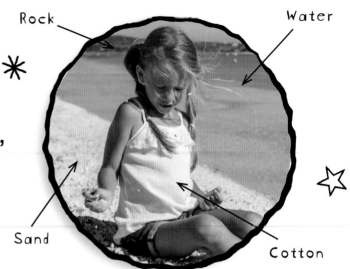

Rock

Water

Sand

Cotton

Without materials, you'd have nothing to sit on, wear or touch. You wouldn't have this book. But that wouldn't matter much, as you wouldn't exist either!

Materials = STUFF

Materials are, quite simply, the **STUFF** that everything is made from. There are millions of different materials, of many types.

Here are just some of them...

Natural materials

Water

Rock

Soil

Gold

Biological materials

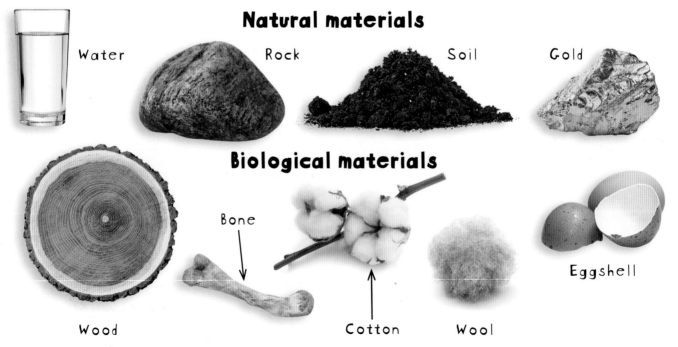

Bone

Eggshell

Wood

Cotton

Wool

Mixed and processed materials

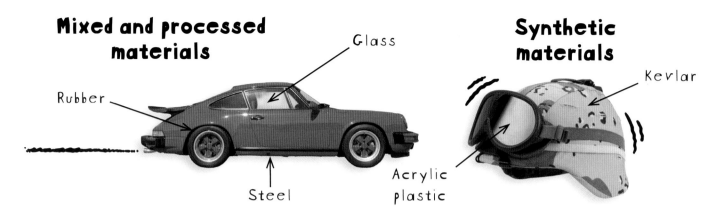

Glass

Rubber

Steel

Acrylic plastic

Synthetic materials

Kevlar

There are several other words you might hear being used to mean materials, or stuff. They include substances, things, objects and matter.

⟹ Matter is the scientific word for stuff!

Scientists also talk about mass, which means the amount of matter in something.

WHAT'S THAT??!

ERM... I THINK IT'S MATTER.

Matter

So, for example, this lump of matter might have a mass of 300 gm.

Material world

Materials make up everything around us: our planet, our homes, our food, even ourselves. So we need to understand how different materials work, change and behave, and what they are useful for, in order to survive.

Since humans first existed, we've been exploring and experimenting with materials to see what they can do and how we can use them – and asking all kinds of questions about them.

This book will try to answer some of them!

What is everything made of?

That's a good question!
(And it's something that you would expect scientists to have discovered by now.)
But it's actually quite hard to answer.

We DO know this much...

AHEM! WE'RE NOT QUITE SURE.

Materials are made of tiny units called atoms.

In a **SOLID**, atoms are tightly packed together and fixed.

In a **LIQUID**, they can move and flow.

In a **GAS**, they are more spread out.

 **Building blocks**

There are different types of atom, and each type forms a pure material, or element. For example, the element gold is made of gold atoms.

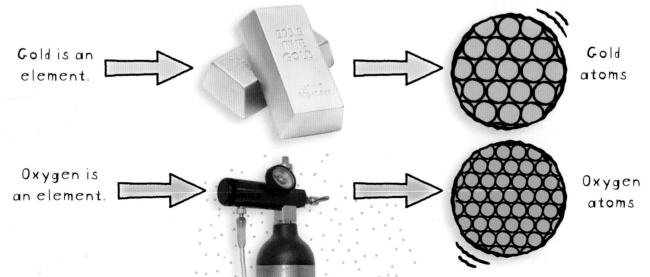

Gold is an element.

Gold atoms

Oxygen is an element.

Oxygen atoms

Compounds

Different atoms can also combine to make molecules, which make up other materials. These materials are called compounds.

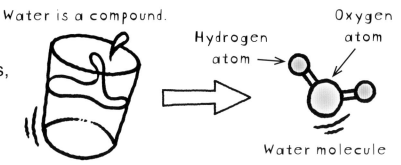

Water is a compound.

Hydrogen atom →

Oxygen atom

Water molecule

Mixture

And elements and compounds can also mix together to make even more materials. A material made of other, mixed materials is called… a mixture!

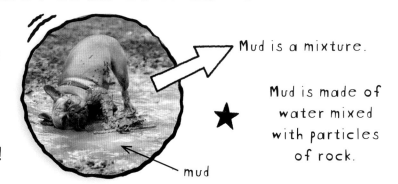

Mud is a mixture.

Mud is made of water mixed with particles of rock.

mud

Smaller and smaller…

Atoms are made of even tinier particles, such as protons and electrons. And they are made of **EVEN** tinier ones, such as quarks and leptons.

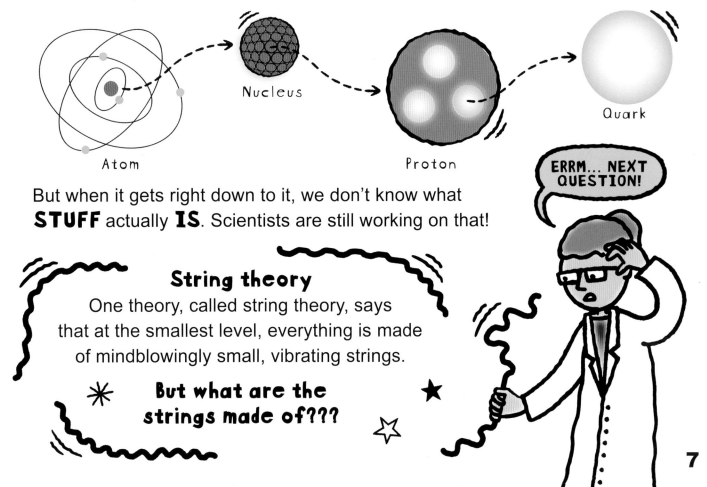

Atom

Nucleus

Proton

Quark

ERRM… NEXT QUESTION!

But when it gets right down to it, we don't know what **STUFF** actually **IS**. Scientists are still working on that!

String theory

One theory, called string theory, says that at the smallest level, everything is made of mindblowingly small, vibrating strings.

But what are the strings made of???

How big are atoms and molecules?

However closely you look at something, you can't see the individual atoms it's made of. That's because they are so INCREDIBLY tiny.

One single atom

Too small to see!

A typical atom is roughly 0.0000001 mm across – or one 10-millionth of a millimetre.

A page in this book is about a million atoms thick.

You could fit about 2,500 million atoms on your little fingernail…

… and a glass of water contains about 24 **SEPTILLION** atoms.

A septillion is a million million million million.

So that's 24,000,000,000,000,000,000,000,000 atoms in a glass of water. That's more than the number of glasses of water in the sea.

Empty space

An atom isn't a solid ball. It has a solid centre, called the nucleus, with tiny parts called electrons zooming around it.

Electron   Nucleus

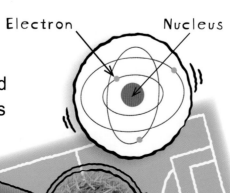

In diagrams like this, the nucleus looks quite big, so that you can see it. But it's actually tiny. If the whole atom was the size of a football stadium…

… the nucleus would be the size of a pea!

You're mostly nothing!

This means that most of an atom is actually not matter. It is a space that's only filled by a cloud of tiny high-energy electrons.

If you could squash all the matter in your body down so that there was no empty space in the atoms, you'd be smaller than a grain of salt.

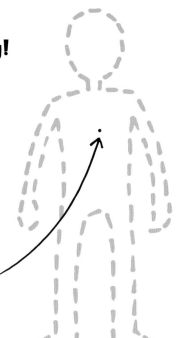

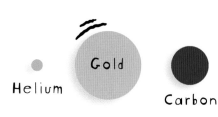

Helium   Gold   Carbon

Big and small

Different types of atom contain different numbers of particles, so some are heavier and bigger than others.

Making molecules

Molecules are made up of atoms joined together. Some are small, like a water molecule, which has three atoms: two hydrogen atoms and one oxygen atom.

Some are bigger, like this molecule of fructose, a type of sugar found in fruit.

This is what makes a strawberry taste sweet!

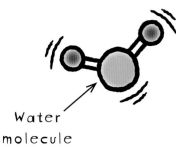

Water molecule

Fructose molecule

What are those sticks for?

Molecule diagrams and models often show the atoms joined together with sticks so you can see them clearly.

In fact, a molecule is more like this, with the atoms squished together.

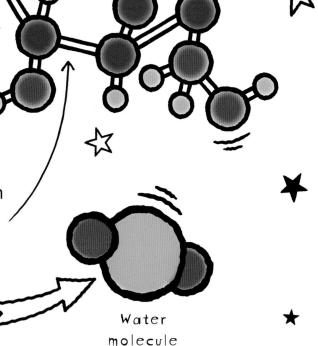

Water molecule

Why is ice slippery?

DON'T FALL OVER!

Materials exist in three main states: **SOLID**, **LIQUID** and GAS.

Ice is water in its solid state. And we all know it can be very slippery.

Ice mystery

We're used to ice being slippery, but finding out why it is hasn't been easy. In fact, for a long time, scientists have got it wrong. Here are the **WRONG** answers!

① Standing on ice makes it melt.

WRONG!

It is true that pressure can lower the freezing temperature of ice and make it start to melt. So scientists thought that standing on ice, in shoes or ice skates, melted the surface into a layer of water, making you slide and slip along. However, it actually takes a **LOT** of pressure to do this – much more than a human's weight. So that's not the answer.

② Friction heats the ice and makes it melt.

WRONG!

Friction happens when surfaces rub together, and it creates heat. (Like when you rub your hands together to warm them up.) So another idea was that skating or sliding around on ice made it melt. This can happen when ice skaters are moving fast. But we all know ice is slippery even when you're standing still. So it's not that either!

And if you think about it, why should ice melting into water make it so slippery? A wet floor or wet rocks can be a bit slippery – but nowhere near as slippery as ice.

So what IS the answer?

Rolling around

The latest theory is that on the surface of ice, some of the molecules it is made of break free.

In ice, water molecules are joined together in a fixed grid or lattice.

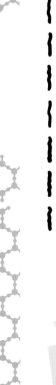

The loose molecules roll and skid around on the surface, like ball bearings on a smooth floor...

WHOOPS!

... making the ice very hard to grip!

But at the surface, some molecules can break off

And did you know?

When ice is REALLY cold, below about -40°C, it's not slippery!

Why is air invisible?

Air is all around us. It's made of gases, and gases are materials. So why can't we see it?

What is a gas?

Gas is one of the three states of matter. The state a material is in depends on its temperature.

Solid

Molecules are fixed together but jiggle around.

Solids keep their shape.

Liquid

Molecules have more energy and move faster.

Liquids can flow and change shape.

Gas

The molecules move so fast that they zoom around at high speeds.

They ping away from each other and spread out.

As a solid gets warmer, it melts into a liquid.

As a liquid gets warmer, it evaporates into a gas.

How hot?

You probably know that water freezes into solid ice at 0°C, and boils into steam (a gas) at 100°C. But other materials change state at other temperatures.

Chocolate melts at about 32°C.

The metal mercury is liquid at room temperature, but freezes solid at about -39°C.

Gases in the air

Air is mostly made of the elements oxygen and nitrogen. At the temperatures we have on Earth, they are normally gases.

Tiny amounts of other gases, such as:
argon
carbon dioxide
and water vapour
(water gas)

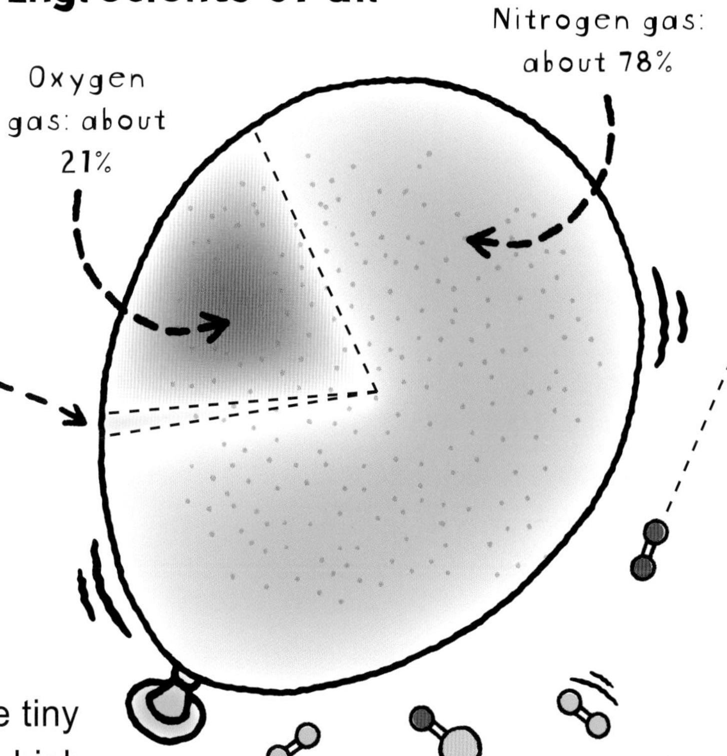

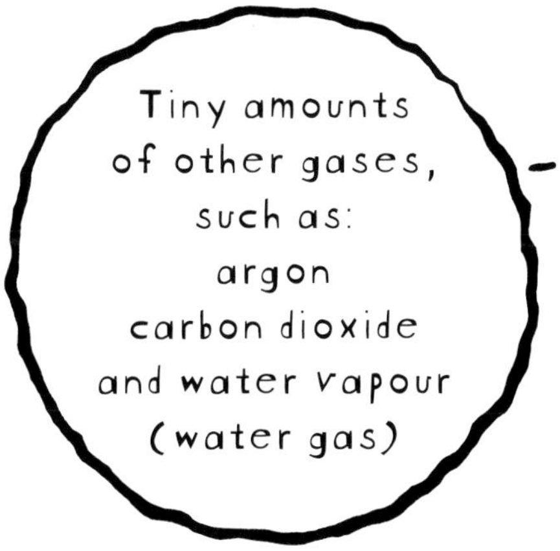

Because they are gases, the tiny molecules zoom around at a high speed, with big spaces in between. Each molecule is too small to see on its own, so the gas is invisible.

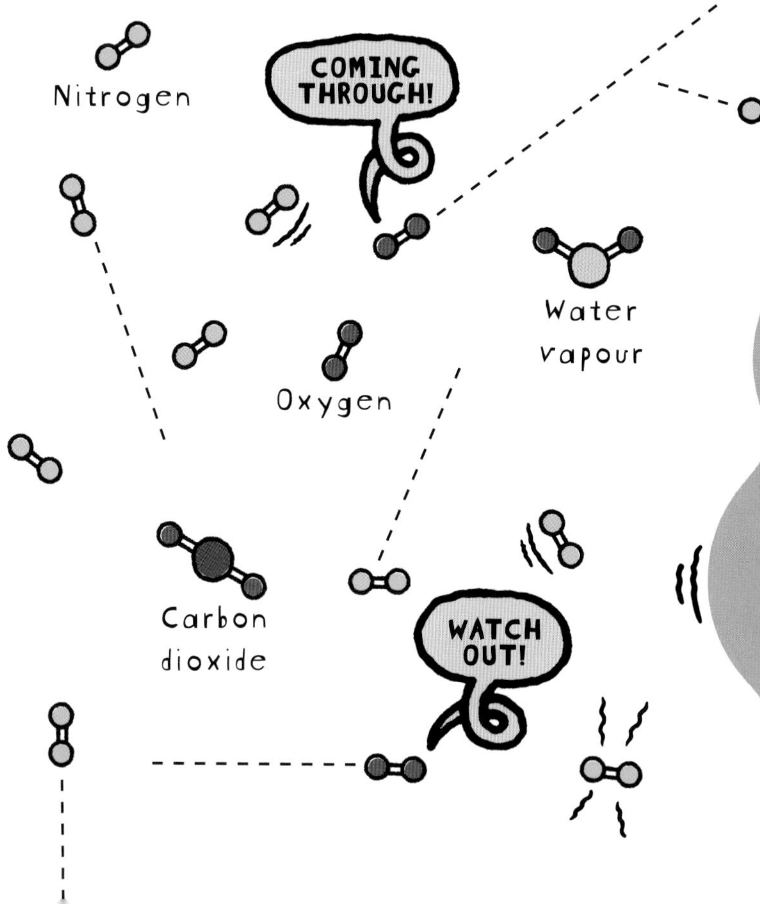

Nitrogen

COMING THROUGH!

Water vapour

Oxygen

Carbon dioxide

WATCH OUT!

Ingredients of air

Oxygen gas: about 21%

Nitrogen gas: about 78%

Solid air

Air can be liquid, and even solid. Liquid air looks like water.

It becomes liquid at a mindbogglingly cold -194.35°C ... and freezes solid at an even chillier -215°C!

Is human hair really as strong as steel?

You might have heard that hair is as strong as steel. That might seem strange, since hair is soft and easy to cut, while steel is used to build skyscrapers and cranes!

In the fairytale, the prince climbs up Rapunzel's hair.

Is hair really strong enough to climb up?

Each material has its own properties – its qualities and what it can do. For example…

IS IT E-L-A-S-T-I-C?

DOES IT FLOAT?

IS IT HARD, SOFT, SMOOTH OR ROUGH?

IS IT WATERPROOF?

HOW STRONG IS IT?

IS IT STIFF OR FLEXIBLE?

IS IT TRANSPARENT?

A material's properties decide what it's useful for – and what it's **NOT** useful for.

Denim makes great jeans, but terrible teapots!

Hair strength test

Strength is an important property, because all kinds of things need to be strong – from buildings and bridges to saucepans and sewing thread.

This strength test measures how much weight a strand of material can hold before it breaks. So materials scientists often do strength tests.

Weights are suspended from the strands to see how much they can hold.

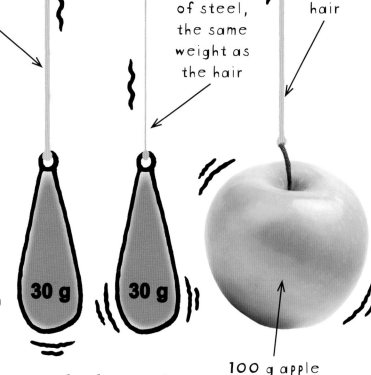

Human hair

Strand of steel, the same weight as the hair

Human hair

30 g

30 g

100 g apple

Which wins?

In this test, the hair would do pretty well. An average human hair can hold about 100 g – the weight of a large apple. It's not quite as strong as steel, but it **IS** as strong as some other metals, such as aluminium.

On average, people have about 100,000 hairs each. If one hair can hold an apple, a whole head of hair could support the weight of two elephants!

(Hair roots are NOT that strong though, so don't try dangling elephants off your hair at home.)

Stretch, don't squish

However, this is only one type of strength, called tensile strength (meaning pulling strength). Scientists also test compressive strength, meaning how strong something is when it's squashed.

On that test, steel is much stronger than human hair.

Why does salt disappear in water?

Put a spoonful of salt into a glass of water, stir it, and –

Ta-daaaa!

It's vanished!

The water looks just like normal water. Try it with a spoonful of sugar too – the same thing happens.

BLEUGH – SALTY!

Taste test

You can prove the sugar and salt are still there by tasting for them. Don't drink the whole glass though, just dip your finger in and dab a bit on your tongue.

MMM – SWEET!

Salt, sugar and many other materials do this because they dissolve in water. The water breaks them down into tiny molecules, or sometimes even atoms.

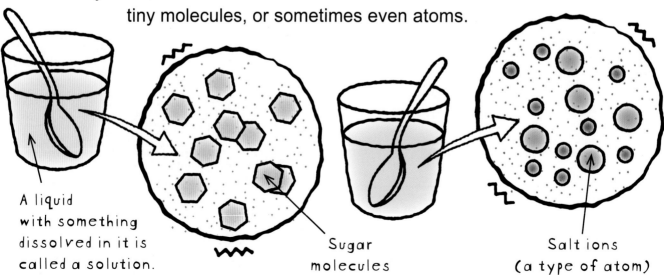

A liquid with something dissolved in it is called a solution.

Sugar molecules

Salt ions (a type of atom)

Does everything dissolve in water?
NO. A lot of materials do dissolve in water, but some don't.

Sugar and salt do.

Some types of rock do, like limestone and chalk.

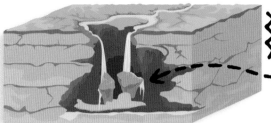

Limestone caves are hollowed out by water dissolving the rock.

Things that don't dissolve in water include candle wax, gold and rubber.

Other solvents
Some things, such as nail polish, don't dissolve in water, but will dissolve in another liquid!

Nail polish will not dissolve in water – so it doesn't come off in the shower or swimming pool.

You can only remove it with nail polish remover. It contains a different solvent, such as ethyl acetate, which dissolves the nail polish.

Get it back!
If you've dissolved salt or sugar in water, you can get it out again.

Pour some of the solution onto a plate or saucer.

Leave it somewhere warm, like a sunny windowsill.

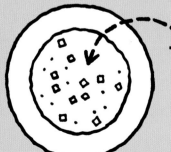

The water will evaporate, leaving the salt or sugar behind.

17

Where do crystals come from?

Crystals include rare and valuable materials, like diamonds – as well as some of the most common materials, like salt, sugar and water ice.

Crystal shapes

In a crystal, the molecules fit together in a pattern that repeats all the way through. This gives the crystal a particular shape, based on the shape of the molecules.

Here's an example... table salt.

Diamonds

Salt molecules are made of two types of atom:

Sodium

Chlorine

Jadeite

They fit together in a cube-shaped molecule...

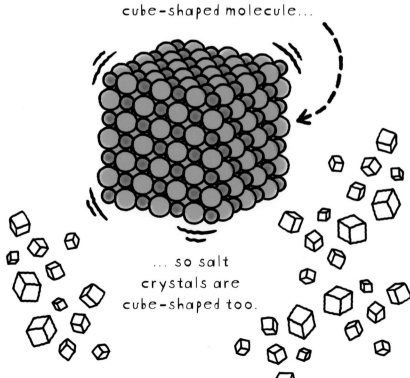

... so salt crystals are cube-shaped too.

Sugar crystals

How can crystals grow?

Crystals aren't alive, but they do grow. This happens when more and more atoms or molecules join onto the crystal in the same pattern.

Crystals can form when rock is melted, then cools again. For example, diamonds grow in melted rock, or magma, deep underground.

Magma

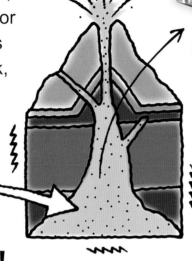

Diamond crystals

Carbon atoms join together in a crystal pattern.

Grow your own!

Crystals can also grow when a material is dissolved in water. You can grow a salt crystal like this:

Stir salt into a jar or jug of hot water until it stops dissolving. Tie a paperclip to a string, tie the other end around a pencil, and hang it into the jar.

Leave it for a few days, and crystals should grow.

Cool crystals

In 2000, miners discovered a cave deep underground, filled with giant selenite crystals up to 12 m long and 4 m wide – as big as a house!

Snowflakes are crystals. They have six points because they grow from six-sided molecules of ice.

When you look through a clear Iceland spar crystal, everything looks double!

19

Why do eggs go solid when you cook them? ☆

As you know, materials can melt into liquid as they heat up, and freeze solid as they get colder. You can see this happening with things like water, butter and chocolate.

But some materials seem to break these rules...

Heat up a runny, liquid egg in a pan...

... and it turns hard and solid!

And what about toast? When you stick bread in a toaster, it doesn't melt.

It just gets darker and crispier.

What's going on?

Materials like bread and egg (and many other foods) contain complicated mixtures of chemicals. When they are heated, they react and change.

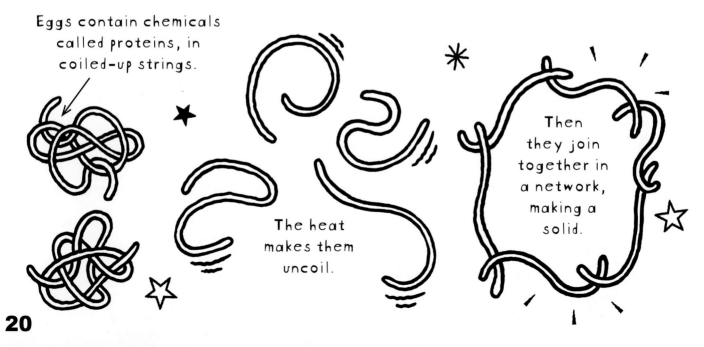

Eggs contain chemicals called proteins, in coiled-up strings.

The heat makes them uncoil.

Then they join together in a network, making a solid.

Bread contains carbohydrate chemicals.

When they get heated, they start to burn, releasing carbon.

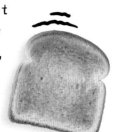

The carbon looks black, so the toast gets darker.

If you kept heating it, it would catch fire!

OUCH!

No going back!

What's more, you can't undo these changes. You can't un-fry an egg or un-toast a slice of bread, because the chemicals have changed permanently. In science, these are called irreversible changes.

Freezing water is a reversible change, because you can undo it.

When you take an ice lolly out of the freezer, the water in it will melt again.

But cooking an egg is an irreversible change.

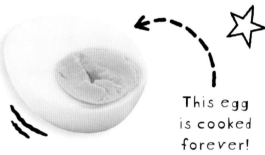

This egg is cooked forever!

The materials in eggs and bread *could* change state and melt, or turn into gas, if they got hot enough. But they don't, because the other changes happen first.

If they didn't, cooking would be very different, as everything would just melt into soup…

IT'S EVERYTHING SOUP AGAIN!

And it's only because things burn that we can make fires, light candles and make engines work by burning fuel.

Why does metal feel cold?

Take a metal spoon out of a kitchen drawer, hold it against your arm, and it feels cold. But a woolly sock feels warm – even if they are exactly the same temperature.

Chilly

Cosy!

FEELS COLD!

Putting your hand in a glass of water

Holding a smooth pebble

Jelly

FEELS WARM!

Wooden spoon

Fluffy cushion

Polystyrene packaging

But WHY?
When you touch a material, you're not actually feeling its temperature. You're just sensing whether your skin is losing or gaining heat.

Here's how it works

① The spoon is at room temperature – about 20°C. Your skin is warmer, as body temperature is about 37°C.

② Metal is very good at conducting heat, or carrying heat through it. When it touches you, heat quickly spreads from your hand into the metal.

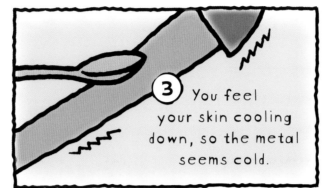

③ You feel your skin cooling down, so the metal seems cold.

④

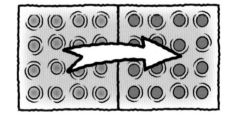

A woolly sock is not good at conducting heat. Instead of carrying heat away, it stops your body heat from escaping, so your skin warms up.

Passing on heat

In hotter materials, the molecules have more energy and move around more.

When a warm material touches a cooler one, its faster molecules hit the slower molecules and make them speed up. That's how heat spreads from one object into another.

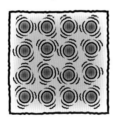

Warm object

Cooler object

Heat spreading

Materials that are good heat conductors quickly 'suck' heat away from your skin, so they make you feel cold.

Good and bad

Metals are very good heat conductors. Water, glass and stone are good conductors too, and so is anything wet, like jelly.

Air is a poor conductor. Materials that feel warm and cosy usually contain trapped air, like a fluffy jumper or polystyrene.

So we make duvets out of soft fabric and fluffy stuffing, not jelly!

SNUGGLY!

What makes the Eiffel Tower grow taller?

Living things, like a sunflower or a kitten, grow. You grow. Even clouds and crystals can grow (see pages 18–19), although they're not alive.

☆ But how can ★ metal grow?

The Eiffel Tower is a famous iron tower in Paris, France. It's 324 m tall – in the winter. But in the summer, especially on a hot day, it can be up to 17 cm taller.

A small piece of iron would only get slightly longer – not enough for you to notice. But a 324-m-tall iron tower expands enough to make a difference you can measure easily.

What's going on!?
This happens because most materials, especially metals, get bigger as they get warmer. It's called heat expansion.

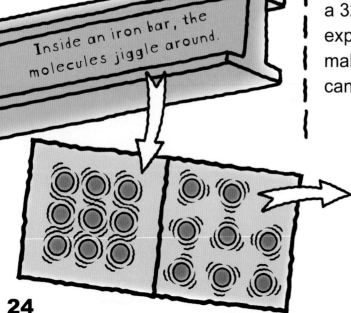

Inside an iron bar, the molecules jiggle around.

As they get hotter, they jiggle more and push against each other more, and the piece of iron grows bigger, or expands.

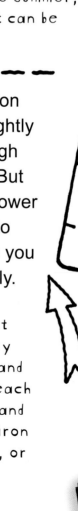

17 cm

Space to grow

It's not so bad for the Eiffel Tower, as it can just grow into the air. But what if a bridge gets longer in the heat?

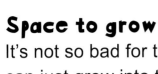

Not good!

Expansion joint

Good!

So bridges and other big structures have gaps built into them, called expansion joints, to let each section grow in the heat.

Liquids and gases

Heat expansion happens in liquids and gases too – in fact, they grow even more than solids. That's how a thermometer works!

A thermometer has liquid inside. As the temperature rises and falls, the liquid expands and shrinks.

Balloon trick

Growing oceans

Global warming is melting ice, which makes sea levels rise. But they also rise because as the seas get warmer, the water expands, and takes up more space.

See air expanding for yourself! Stretch a balloon over the neck of an empty plastic bottle. Then hold the bottle in a bowl of hot tap water.

The air inside expands, and fills the balloon.

Do plastic bags last forever?

As you probably know, plastic bags are a BIG problem. Many end up as litter on the land and in the sea – where they stay for a long, long time.

Sea creatures can die when they swallow plastic bags, mistaking them for food such as jellyfish.

How long do they last?

It's hard to be sure, because plastic was only invented about 150 years ago. It's incredibly long-lasting, and doesn't break down and rot away, like natural materials do. So we're not sure how long plastic bags might last. It could be thousands of years!

A lot of rot

When things rot, or biodegrade, they are actually being eaten and digested by bacteria, which turn them into natural chemicals.

An apple rots after a few days.

Wood eventually decays.

Plastic bags don't!

Why doesn't it rot?

Plastic is a synthetic material, meaning it's made by humans. It's made from natural materials, usually oil from under the ground.

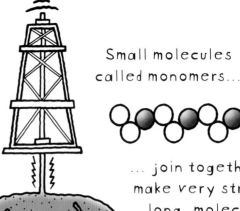

Oil is a fossil fuel made from the bodies of tiny ancient animals.

To make plastic, we take chemicals out of the oil and heat them up so that their molecules change.

Small molecules called monomers...

... join together to make very strong, long, molecule chains called polymers.

The GOOD NEWS is...

As a material, plastic has amazingly useful properties.

Flexible

*

Cheap

Waterproof

*

Strong

Long-lasting

*

Light

That's why we use it so much!

The BAD NEWS is...

The polymer molecules in plastic are too big and strong for bacteria to digest. That's why it doesn't break down and rot away. It can break up into smaller pieces – but they're still plastic, and harm animals and the environment.

What can we do?

HELP!

☆ **Invent alternative plastics that do rot away.**

☆ **Find ways to collect and clean up waste plastic.**

Breed bacteria that can digest plastic.

Meanwhile, it's a good idea to avoid using plastic if you can – especially plastic bags!

Quick-fire questions

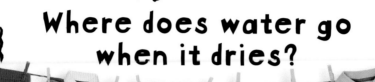

Where does water go when it dries?

The water in a puddle in the sunshine, or in washing hung up to dry, gradually disappears until it's all gone. Water turns into a gas when it boils, but even when it's not boiling, water molecules gradually break free into the air and become water vapour (water gas). The warmer it is, the faster the water molecules move and the more easily they break away, so things dry faster.

Why does ice float?

Most materials expand or grow as they get warmer, and shrink as they get colder. However, water is different. Below 4°C, water stops shrinking as it cools, and starts to grow again. Its molecules move away from each other slightly to form ice crystals. This means ice is less dense (lighter for its size) than liquid water, so it floats.

If lead is poisonous, why is it used in pencils?

Lead is a poisonous metal that can be very dangerous if you swallow it or breathe it into your lungs. However, the 'lead' in pencils is not made of lead – it's made of graphite, a type of carbon (like the black stuff on burnt toast). It's called lead because it looks similar, and when it was first discovered, people thought graphite was a type of lead.

How can trousers be made of wood?

The fabrics we use to make clothes come from many different sources. Cotton and linen plants and animal wool have fibres that can be woven into cloth. We can also make cloth fibres from plastic. And some are made by processing wood or bamboo, which results in fabrics such as rayon and viscose.

How do clouds stay up?

Clouds are made of water, which of course is denser than air and doesn't float. But when water is a gas, its molecules are separate and zoom around very fast, just like all the other gases in the air. As the air cools, the water molecules start to condense, and stick together to make larger droplets – but they are still light enough to stay in the air.

Glossary

Atoms Tiny units that matter is made up of.

Bacteria Tiny living things that feed on some types of matter.

Biological To do with living things.

Carbon An important element found in living things.

Carbon dioxide A gas found in the air.

Compound A material made from atoms of different elements joined together to form molecules.

Conductor A material that conducts or carries heat through it easily.

Crystal A material with its atoms or molecules arranged in a regular repeating grid or lattice.

Density How heavy something is for its size.

Dissolve To break up and disappear into a liquid, such as water.

Electrons Tiny parts of atoms.

Elements Pure materials made of one type of atom, and the building blocks of matter.

Evaporate To change from a liquid into a gas.

Friction A force that slows down or stops objects as they scrape or rub together.

Heat expansion The way most materials expand or get bigger as they get warmer.

Hydrogen A common element, and one of the two ingredients of water.

Ion An atom or molecule with an electric charge.

Irreversible change A change to a material that cannot be reversed or undone, such as cooking an egg.

Lattice A regular pattern or grid of molecules found in some materials, especially crystals.

Mass The amount of matter that an object contains.

Matter The stuff that everything is made up of.

Mixture A material made of different elements or compounds mixed together.

Molecules Units of matter made from atoms joined together.

Monomers Small single molecules that can join together to make larger molecules.

Nitrogen An element usually found as a gas, that makes up most of the air.

Nucleus The solid central part of an atom.

Oxygen A gas found in the air, and one of the two ingredients of water.

Polymer A type of molecule made of a chain of monomers, and found in plastics.

Reversible change A change to a material that can be reversed or undone, such as freezing water.

Solution A liquid with another material dissolved in it.

States of matter The three main states that materials can exist in: solid, liquid and gas.

Water vapour Water in the form of a gas.

Further reading

Websites

www.exploratorium.edu/snacks/subject/materials-and-matter
Matter and materials experiments from the Exploratorium.

www.dkfindout.com/uk/science/materials/
Matter and materials facts, pictures and quizzes.

phet.colorado.edu/sims/html/states-of-matter/latest/states-of-matter_en.html
Interactive animation that lets you heat and cool materials to see what happens.

www.stevespanglerscience.com/lab/categories/experiments states-of-matter/
States of matter experiments from Steve Spangler Science.

pt.kle.cz/en_US/index.html
The periodic table, a table showing all the elements.
Click on each one to find out about it.

Books

Working with Materials
by Sonya Newland (Wayland, 2020)

The Solid Truth about States of Matter with Max Axiom, Super Scientist
by Agnieszka Biskup (Capstone Press, 2019)

See inside Atoms and Molecules
by Rosie Dickens (Usborne Publishing, 2020)

Making with States of Matter
by Anna Claybourne (Wayland, 2019)

The Element in the Room
by Mike Bardfield (Laurence King, 2018)

Index

A Question of Science titles:

978 1 4451 1162 7 HB
978 1 4451 1163 4 PB

What are animals?
How can a snake swallow an antelope?
Why don't cats lay eggs?
Why don't caterpillars look
like their parents?
Why can't animals talk to us?
Why can't penguins fly?
Which is the cleverest animal
How do chameleons change colour?
What are camels' humps made of?
How can a cockroach live
without its head?
What happened to the dinosaurs?

978 1 4451 1161 0 HB
978 1 4451 1160 3 PB

What is electricity?
How do we make electricity?
Where does electricity come from?
Why do shopping trolleys zap you?
Where does lightning come from?
Why doesn't electricity
leak out of sockets?
Why are electric wires
covered in plastic?
Did people have electricity
in ancient times?
Is an electric eel really electric?
Can electricity bring something
dead back to life?
Will we run out of electricity?
How fast can an electric car go?

978 1 4451 1154 2 HB
978 1 4451 1155 9 PB

How do our bodies work?
Why can't people fly?
Why don't your eyeballs fall out?
Why is blood red?
Why do germs make you ill?
Why do I have to eat sprouts?
What are hiccups?
What is poo made of?
How fast can a human go?
Why do children's teeth fall out?
Where do you keep your memories?
What are bellybuttons for?

978 1 5263 1136 8 HB
978 1 5263 1137 5 PB

What is a force?
Why doesn't the Moon fall down?
Why does rubbing your hands
together warm them up?
Why don't pond-skaters fall in?
How does a parachute
save your life?
How can a metal boat float?
How can a plane fly upside down?
Why can't people grow
as big as dinosaurs?
Why is falling off a cliff so deadly?
How can a magnet pull something
it's not touching?
How does the tablecloth trick work?
Why can you jump higher
on the Moon?

978 1 4451 1156 6 HB
978 1 4451 1157 3 PB

What is light?
Where does light go when
you switch it off?
Why does a mirror show things
back to front?
Why does the Moon shine?
How can your shadow be taller
than you?
How can binoculars make
things look closer?
Where do the stars go
in the daytime?
What makes things different colours?
Why can't you ever reach a rainbow?
How does light get inside your eyes?
How can an X-ray see through you?
Is an invisibility cloak possible?

978 1 4451 1164 1 HB
978 1 4451 1165 8 PB

What are materials?
Why is ice slippery?
What is everything made of?
How big are atoms and molecules?
Why is air invisible?
Is human hair as strong as steel?
Why does salt disappear in water?
Where do crystals come from?
Why do eggs go solid when
you cook them?
Why does metal feel cold?
What makes the Eiffel Tower grow taller?
Do plastic bags last forever?

978 1 4451 1158 0 HB
978 1 4451 1159 7 PB

What are plants?
Why don't plants have mouths?
Could we exist without plants?
Why can't plants walk around?
How do cactuses survive
in the desert?
Why do flowers smell nice?
How can a seed grow after
thousands of years?
Do plants have feelings?
Why are trees so big?
Can plants talk to each other?
Could a plant eat a person?
Are there plants on other planets?

978 1 4451 1257 0 HB
978 1 4451 1256 3 PB

What is sound?
How do sounds get inside your ears?
Can you hear sounds in space?
Why can't you see sound waves?
How fast is a supersonic plane?
What was the loudest sound ever?
Why do lions roar but mice squeak?
Where do sound waves go?
Why is it hard to hear underwater?
Can deaf people feel sounds?
Can a sound kill you?
Which animal has the best hearing?